# Broccoli
# and
# Bubble Gum

**Illustrations by Greg Nemec
and Randy Messer**

**Edited by
Jeffrey Copeland**

# Contents

# Broccoli and Bubble Gum

Will You?

## Will You?

What kind of creature will you be?
Will you dig with your claws?
Will you hang from a tree?

Will you sniff at the ground?
Catch a bug for lunch?
Scratch yourself all around?

Will you crawl near the shore?
Will you snort or grunt?
Will you howl or roar?

Or will you quietly hiss
      like
         this s s s s s s s s s s s s ?

Eve Merriam

# Writing Wizard

Pretend you have just discovered a strange new creature. Write what you would say about this creature in a TV news report.

Will You?

# Pint-Sized Poet

Write a diamante (a poem in the shape of a diamond) about the kind of creature you would like to be.

**Directions:**

On line 2, write two words that describe the creature you would like to be.

On line 3, write three words that describe the way the creature moves.

On line 4, write two words that describe how this creature would make others feel.

1. Creature

2. _____  _____

3. _____ _____ _____

4. _____  _____

5. Me

**Diamante (Form)**

## All-Around Artist

Will You?

Draw a picture of an imaginary animal that you would like to be.

# Broccoli and Bubble Gum

## School,
## Some Suggestions

If kids could be the teachers,
If kids could make the rules,
There'd be a lot of changes made
In almost all the schools.
First thing they'd stop the homework.
They'd never give a test.
They know that growing children
Must have their proper rest.
They'd make the lunchtime longer—
Let's say from twelve to two,
So every growing boy or girl
Had time enough to chew!

Of course, concerning recess,
Kids clearly realize
To keep his body healthy,
A child needs exercise.
And so there would be recess,
Perhaps from nine to ten,
And then when it is two o'clock,
It's recess time again!
With longer, stronger weekends,
Each child would grow so smart
He would perform with excellence
In music, gym, and art!

Bobbi Katz

# Writing Wizard

Write a suggestion you would like to make to the
principal of your school.

_____

_____

_____

_____

_____

_____

# Pint-Sized Poet

Write a poem about your school.
When you finish, you will have a
poem with three stanzas.

My school has lots of _____
(noun)

and lots of _____ to do!
(noun)

Kids like to _____ and _____ each day
(action word)                    (action word)

with _____ and _____ , it's true.
(noun)                    (noun)

If kids could make the rules,

**Stanza**      we'd have lots of _____ , too!
(noun)

## All-Around Artist

Draw a picture of something you would like to see
added to your school.

School, Some Suggestions

# Broccoli and Bubble Gum

## Darling Little Esmerilla

Darling little Esmerilla
Was a furry caterpillar.
Her home was in a little wood,
And she was happy, quiet and good.
She caused no creature any harm,
And lived a life of gentle charm.
The only thing that she did wrong
Was dreaming as she crawled along.
She did not look where she was going,
But wandered where the wind was blowing,
As free and easy as a feather.
*She was too careless altogether.*

She once gave me a dreadful fright
When, glancing neither left nor right,
And very difficult to see,
She crossed my path in front of me.
I only saw her, small and brown,
Just before my foot came down.
And oh, I'm glad I did not kill her.
That lovely furry caterpillar!

BE SENSIBLE AND IF YOU TRY
YOU MAY BECOME A BUTTERFLY.

Charlotte Hough

## Writing Wizard

Imagine you are Esmerilla. Write what you would dream about on the lines inside the balloon.

### Darling Little Esmerilla

## Pint-Sized Poet

Write a poem about a beautiful butterfly.

**Directions:**
   On line 2, write two words that describe a butterfly.
   On line 3, write two words that tell what a butterfly does.
   On line 4, write the name of something pretty.

1. Butterfly

2. _____ and _____

3. _____ _____

4. Pretty as a _____

5. Butterfly

**Simile**

## All-Around Artist

Draw a picture of Esmerilla as a beautiful butterfly.

# Broccoli and Bubble Gum

### If You've Never

## If You've Never

If you've never seen an old witch
Riding through the sky—
Or never felt big bat's wings
Flopping, as they fly—
If you've never touched a white thing
Gliding through the air,
And knew it was a ghost because
You got a dreadful scare—
If you've never heard the night owls,
Crying, "Whoo-whoo-whoo?"
And never jumped at pumpkin eyes
Gleaming out at you—
If all of these exciting things
You've never heard nor seen,
Why then—you've missed a lot of fun,
Because—that's HALLOWE'EN!

Elsie M. Fowler

# Writing Wizard

Write a scary letter to someone you know, but don't sign your name. Warn that person about something that could happen on Halloween night!

Date _____

Dear _____,

This is a warning! _____

_____

_____

_____

Anonymously yours,

# Pint-Sized Poet

Circle the face below that shows the feeling you had when you read the poem.

**Mood (Tone)**

## All-Around Artist

Draw a picture of a scary Halloween creature.

If You've Never

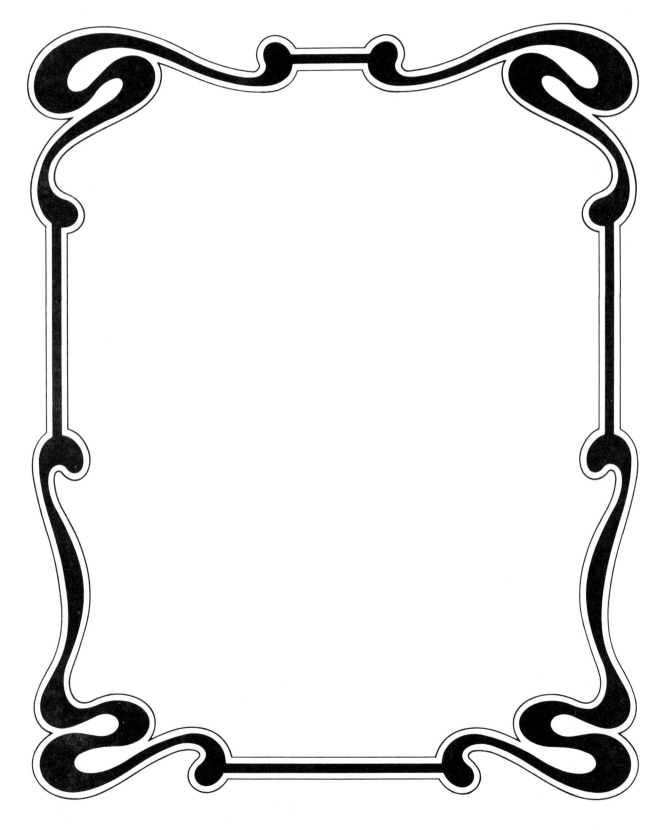

# Broccoli and Bubble Gum

## The Mouse in the Stew

### The Mouse in the Stew

A youngster while dining at Crewe,
Found quite a large mouse in his stew.
    Said the waiter, "Don't shout,
    And wave it about,
Or the rest will be wanting one, too."

Anonymous

## Writing Wizard

The Mouse in the Stew

If you could be a mouse for one day, where would you go and what would you eat?

## Pint-Sized Poet

Write your own limerick. A
*limerick* is a silly poem with five
lines that rhyme.

There once was a _____ named Pete,

Who refused to eat any meat.

He ate _____ and tomatoes,

_____ and potatoes,

And anything made out of wheat!

**Limerick (Form)**

## All-Around Artist

The Mouse in the Stew

Draw a picture of the mouse in the poem cooking a meal for the customers.

Bubble Gum

## Bubble Gum

I'm in trouble
made a bubble
peeled it off my nose

Felt a rock
inside my sock
got gum between my toes

Made another
told my brother
we could blow a pair

Give three cheers
now our ears
are sticking to our hair.

Nina Payne

## Writing Wizard

Design a wrapper for a terrific new bubble gum.

Bubble Gum

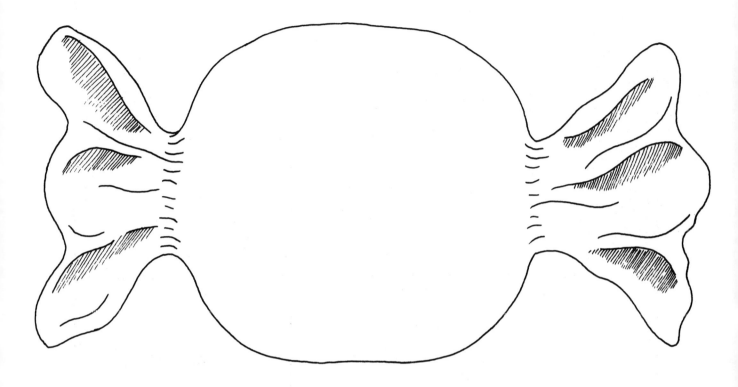

## Pint-Sized Poet

Draw a line under the word that rhymes with trouble.
Draw a circle around the word that rhymes with nose.
Draw a box around the word that rhymes with rock.

I'm in <u>trouble</u>

made a bubble

peeled it off my (nose)

Felt a [rock]

inside my sock

got gum between my toes.

**Rhyme**

## All-Around Artist

Bubble Gum

Draw a picture of someone blowing a bubble in an
unusual shape.

# Broccoli and Bubble Gum

## Jump—jump—jump

Jump—jump—jump—
  Jump away
From this town into
  The next, to-day.

Jump—jump—jump—
  Jump over the moon;
Jump all the morning,
  And all the noon.

Jump—jump—jump—
  Jump all night;
Won't our mothers
  Be in a fright?

Jump—jump—jump—
  Over the sea;
What wonderful wonders
  We shall see.

Jump—jump—jump—
  Jump far away;
And all come home
  Some other day.

Kate Greenaway

# Writing Wizard

## Jump—jump—jump

Pretend you are the kid in the poem. Send a postcard to your parents. Tell them what you have seen on your jumping trip. Let them know where you are going next and when you will be home.

STAMP

# Pint-Sized Poet

Think of an action word other than the word *jump*. Write your new word on each blank. Read your poem aloud to see how it sounds.

_____ — _____ — _____

_____ away

From this town into

The next, to-day.

_____ — _____ — _____

_____ over the moon;

_____ all the morning,

**Repetition**

And all the noon.

## All-Around Artist

Jump—jump—jump

Draw a picture of an animal that is a good jumper.

# Broccoli and Bubble Gum

## When It Rains

"Quack, quack, quack!" says the little white duck.
"Here comes the rain—and I'm in luck.
I don't have to bother with overshoes,
I can splash in the puddles where I choose."

"Oink, oink, oink!" squeals the little red pig.
"Now there'll be plenty of mud to dig.
A fine pig-wallow I'd like to see,
If it rains all day, it will just suit me."

"Boom, boom, boom!" says the big green frog.
"There's no better home than a nice wet bog.
It takes rainy weather to keep it cool
And fill my favorite diving pool."

"Rain, rain, rain!" sigh Jackie and Jill
With elbows propped on the window sill.
Then one gives a whoop, and the other a shout,
The sun and a rainbow have both popped out!

May Justus

## Writing Wizard

Imagine you are writing a book of activities for little kids.
Write a list of fun things to do on a rainy day.

Rainy Day Activities

1. _____

2. _____

3. _____

4. _____

5. _____

## Pint-Sized Poet

Write a poem about sounds things
make. Read your poem aloud.
Listen to the sounds.

_____ bang.

Bells _____ .

_____ snap.

Shoes _____ .

_____ squeak.

Old stairs _____ .

A _____ chops.

**Onomatopoeia**

Popcorn _____ .

## All-Around Artist

Draw a picture of one of the animals in the poem playing in the rain.

When It Rains

# Broccoli and Bubble Gum

## Candy Apples

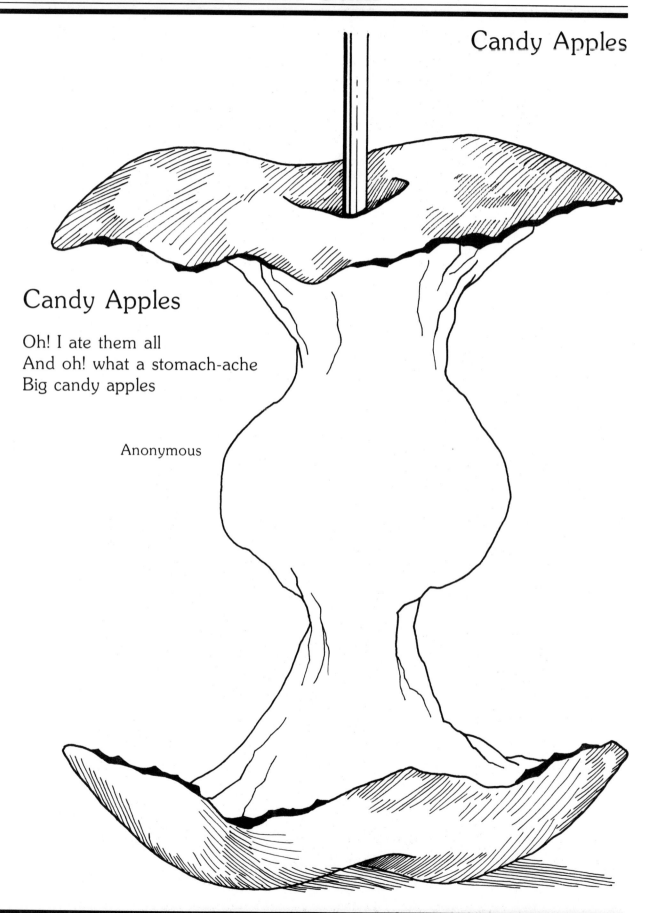

## Candy Apples

Oh! I ate them all
And oh! what a stomach-ache
Big candy apples

Anonymous

## Writing Wizard

Pretend you are selling candy apples at the fair. Write a sign that will make everyone want to buy your candy apples.

Candy Apples

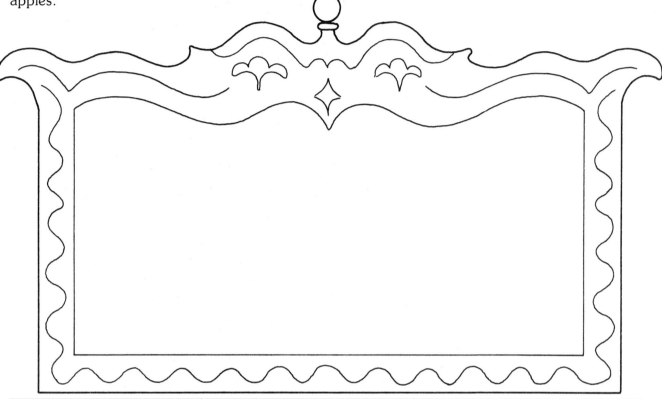

## Pint-Sized Poet

Write a haiku about an animal you might see at the fair. A *haiku* is a little poem with three lines that describes something you can see, smell, hear, taste, or touch. Write one or two words on each line.

A _____ walked proudly
(animal)

To the judges' _____
(noun)

To receive the _____
(noun)

**Haiku (Form)**

## All-Around Artist

Draw a picture of yourself eating a candy apple at an
amusement park or fair.

Candy Apples

# Broccoli and Bubble Gum

## Between Birthdays

My birthdays take so long to start.
They come along a year apart.
It's worse than waiting for a bus;
I fear I used to fret and fuss,
But now, when by impatience vexed
Between one birthday and the next,
I think of all that I have seen
That keeps on happening in between.
The songs I've heard, the things I've done,
Make my un-birthdays not so un-

Ogden Nash

## Writing Wizard

Write three important things that you have seen, heard, or done since your last birthday.

## Pint-Sized Poet

Poems often have a special rhythm or beat. Each word or word part that is underlined counts as one beat. Count the beats in each line. Write the number of beats in the box at the end of each line.

My birth days take so long to start. ☐

They come a long a year a part. ☐

It's worse than wait ing for a bus; ☐

I fear I used to fret and fuss. ☐

Now write your own special line of poetry and count the beats.

_____ ☐

**Rhythm**

## All-Around Artist

Draw a picture of what you think you will look like in
ten years.

Between Birthdays

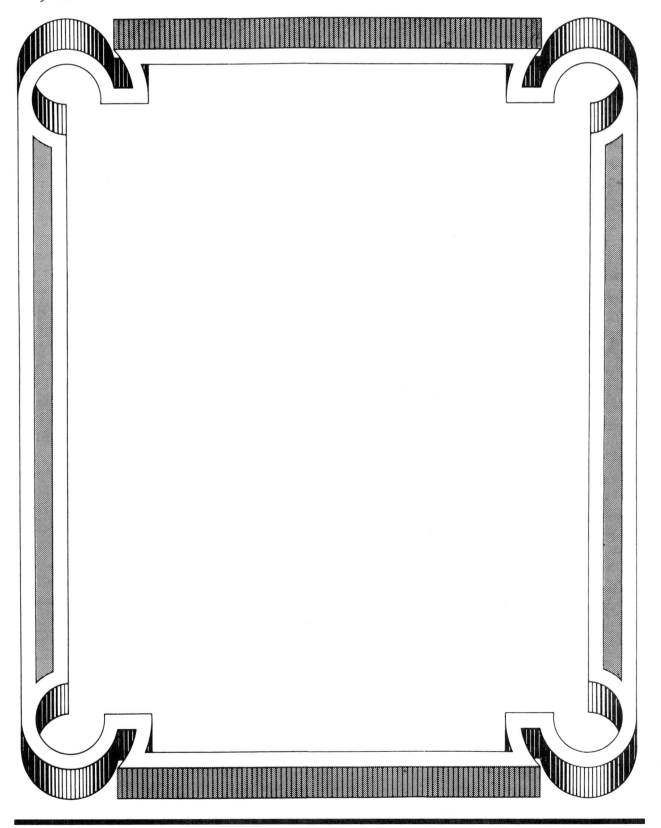

# Broccoli and Bubble Gum

Sunflakes

## Sunflakes

If sunlight fell like snowflakes,
gleaming yellow and so bright,
we could build a sunman,
we could have a sunball fight,
we could watch the sunflakes
drifting in the sky.
We could go sleighing
in the middle of July
through sundrifts and sunbanks,
we could ride a sunmobile,
and we could touch sunflakes—
I wonder how they'd feel.

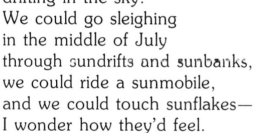

Frank Asch

# Writing Wizard

Pretend you are on a special vacation in a place where sunlight falls like snowflakes. Write a letter to a friend. Tell your friend about this amazing place!

Date _____

Dear _____ ,

_____

_____

_____

_____

Your friend,

_____

# Pint-Sized Poet

Write a diamante (a poem in the shape of a diamond) about sunflakes.

**Directions:**
   On line 2, write two words that describe what sunflakes look like.
   On line 3, write three words that describe what sunflakes do.
   On line 4, write two words that describe how sunflakes make you feel.

1. Sunflakes

2. _____  _____

3. _____  _____  _____

4. _____  _____

5. Sunflakes

**Diamante (Form)**

# All-Around Artist

Draw a picture of yourself playing in sunflakes.

Sunflakes

# Broccoli and Bubble Gum

Skating

## Skating

When I try to skate,
My feet are so wary
They grit and they grate;
And then I watch Mary
Easily gliding,
Like an ice-fairy;
Skimming and curving,
Out and in,
With a turn of her head,
And a lift of her chin,
And a gleam of her eye,
And a twirl and a spin;
Sailing under
The breathless hush
Of the willows, and back
To the frozen rush;
Out to the island
And round the edge,
Skirting the rim
Of the crackling sedge,

**Broccoli and Bubble Gum**

# Skating

Swerving close
To the poplar root,
And round the lake
On a single foot,
With a three, and an eight,
And a loop and a ring;
Where Mary glides,
The lake will sing!
Out in the mist
I hear her now
Under the frost
Of the willow-bough
Easily sailing,
Light and fleet,
With the song of the lake
Beneath her feet.

Herbert Asquith

# Writing Wizard

Write a story about a pair of magic ice skates.

# Pint-Sized Poet

Finish this poem about skating.
Write one or two words on each
line.

I skate as fast as a _____

On ice as smooth as _____ .

My skates are as sharp as _____ .

I feel as free as _____ .

**Simile**

# All-Around Artist

**Skating**

Draw a picture of yourself enjoying your favorite winter activity.

# Broccoli and Bubble Gum

## Fish

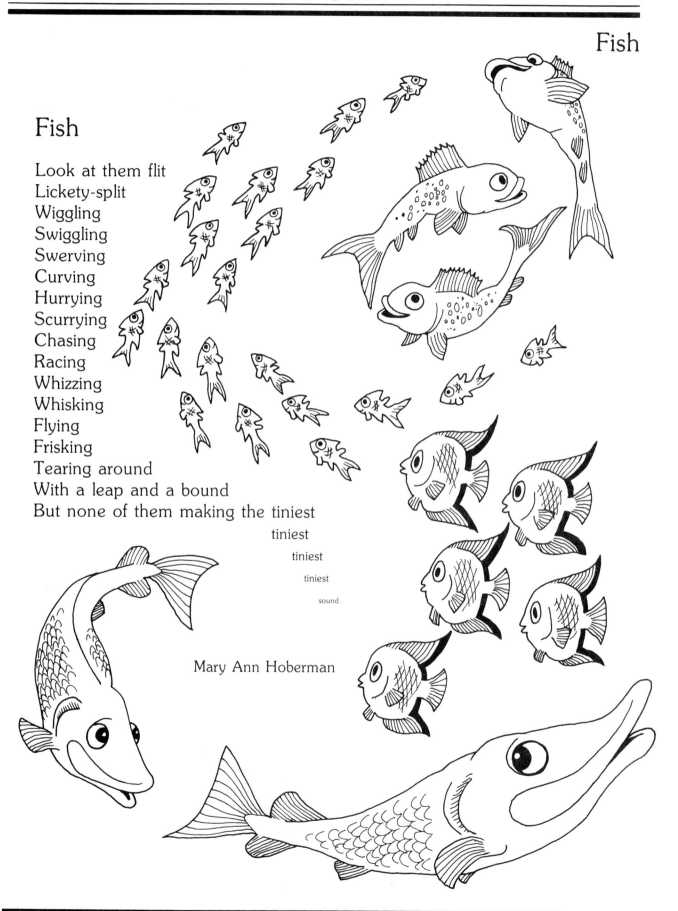

Look at them flit
Lickety-split
Wiggling
Swiggling
Swerving
Curving
Hurrying
Scurrying
Chasing
Racing
Whizzing
Whisking
Flying
Frisking
Tearing around
With a leap and a bound
But none of them making the tiniest
               tiniest
                  tiniest
                    tiniest
                      sound.

Mary Ann Hoberman

## Writing Wizard

Fish

Imagine you are a deep-sea diver. Write about something exciting that you saw today.

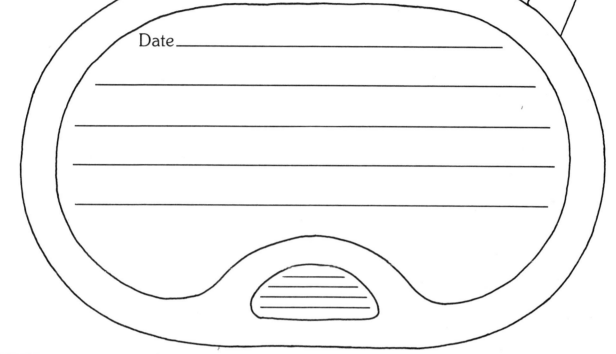

Date _____

## Pint-Sized Poet

Some poems have unusual shapes. Write a poem in the shape of a fish. Around the edge of the fish shape, write words that describe a fish.

**Shape (Form)**

## All-Around Artist

Draw a picture of several fish having a party at the bottom of the sea.

Fish

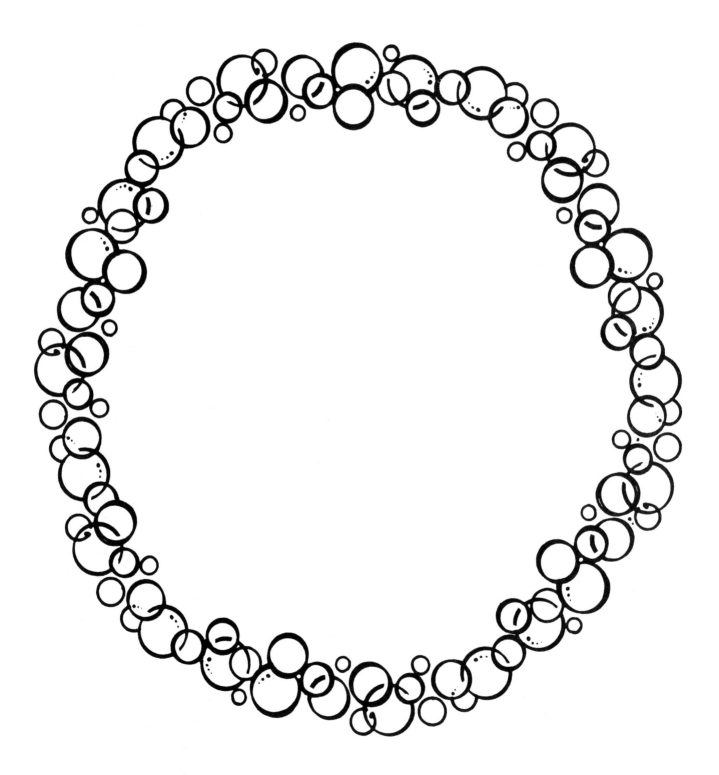

# Broccoli and Bubble Gum

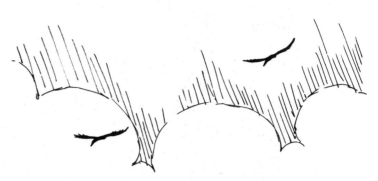

## Treasure Hunting

"Look!" said Tommy,
"Look!" cried he.
"See what I've found—
This funny old key!"
A funny old key,
Buried in the sand.
Dropped, maybe,
From a pirate's hand.
Dropped from his hand
On the very day
He was hiding,
His gold away.
While he was hiding
His gold in a box—
This was the key
To the big brass locks.
"Listen," said Tommy,
"Listen," said he,
"Let's find the treasure
Buried by the sea.
Half will be mine,
Half will go to you."
"Yes," I agreed.
"That's the thing to do."
When Tommy goes treasure hunting
I go, too.

May Justus

## Writing Wizard

Write a story about going on a treasure hunt with a friend.

Treasure Hunting

## Pint-Sized Poet

Write a poem about going on a treasure hunt.

**Directions:**
   On line 2, write two words that describe what treasure hunting is like.
   On line 3, write two words that tell what a treasure looks like.
   On line 4, write two words that tell how you feel about treasure hunting.

1. Treasure

2. _____ and _____

3. _____ _____

4. _____ _____

5. Pirate's Chest

**Imagery**

## All-Around Artist

Draw a map that shows where a treasure is buried.

Treasure Hunting

# Broccoli and Bubble Gum

Merry Tinkle

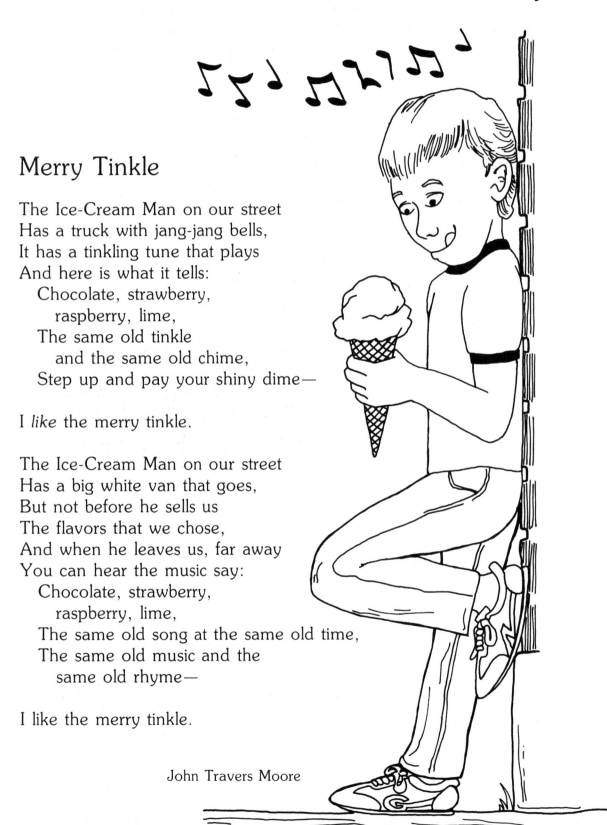

## Merry Tinkle

The Ice-Cream Man on our street
Has a truck with jang-jang bells,
It has a tinkling tune that plays
And here is what it tells:
   Chocolate, strawberry,
     raspberry, lime,
   The same old tinkle
     and the same old chime,
   Step up and pay your shiny dime—

I *like* the merry tinkle.

The Ice-Cream Man on our street
Has a big white van that goes,
But not before he sells us
The flavors that we chose,
And when he leaves us, far away
You can hear the music say:
   Chocolate, strawberry,
     raspberry, lime,
   The same old song at the same old time,
   The same old music and the
     same old rhyme—

I like the merry tinkle.

John Travers Moore

# Writing Wizard

Merry Tinkle

Imagine the Ice-Cream Man has a new ice-cream treat he wants you to try. Write the name of the treat and describe what you like or dislike about it.

# Pint-Sized Poet

Think of what you would hear if an ice-cream truck came by. Write what you would hear on each blank.

" _____ ,"

" _____ ,"
(repeat the word above)

That's what the kids all hear.

" _____ ,"
(repeat the word above)

" _____ ,"
(repeat the word above)

The Ice-Cream Man is near!

**Repetition**

# All-Around Artist

Draw a picture of your favorite ice-cream treat.

# Broccoli and Bubble Gum

Spaghetti! Spaghetti!

## Spaghetti! Spaghetti!

Spaghetti! spaghetti!
you're wonderful stuff,
I love you, spaghetti,
I can't get enough.
You're covered with sauce
and you're sprinkled with cheese,
spaghetti! spaghetti!
oh, give me some please.

Spaghetti! spaghetti!
piled high in a mound,
you wiggle, you wriggle,
you squiggle around.
There's slurpy spaghetti
all over my plate,
spaghetti! spaghetti!
I think you are great.

Jack Prelutsky

## Writing Wizard

Spaghetti! Spaghetti!

Write your own special recipe for spaghetti.

Ingredients: _____ _____

_____ _____

_____ _____

Cooking Instructions: _____

_____

_____

_____

_____

## Pint-Sized Poet

Circle the face below that shows the feeling you had when you read this poem.

**Mood (Tone)**

## All-Around Artist

Draw a picture of you and your friends in a spaghetti-eating contest.

Spaghetti! Spaghetti!

# Broccoli and Bubble Gum

## Oh the Toe-Test!

## Oh the Toe-Test!

The fly, the fly,
in the wink of an eye,
can taste with his feet
if the syrup is sweet
or the bacon is salty.
Oh is it his fault he
gets toast on his toes
as he tastes as he goes?

Norma Farber

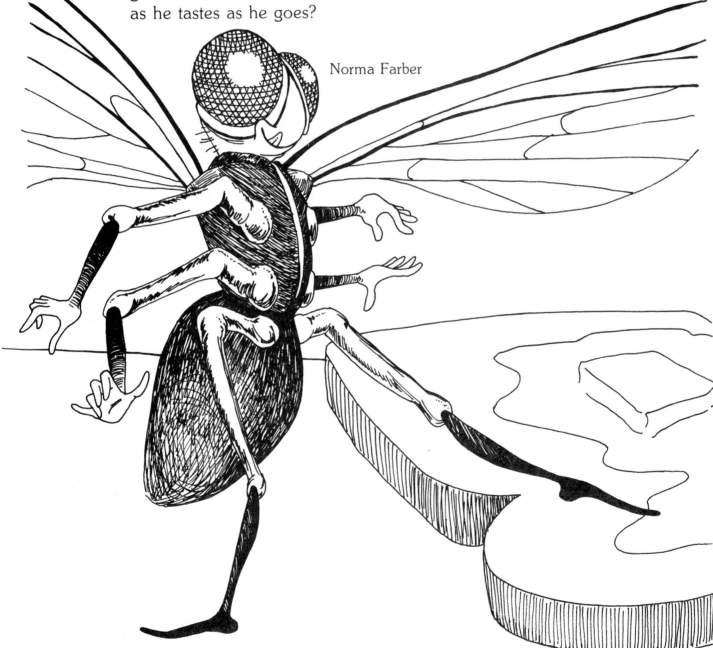

## Writing Wizard

Imagine you are the fly in the poem and you are looking for a job. Fill out the application below for a job as a food taster.

Oh the Toe-Test!

**Position: Food Taster**

Name: _____

Previous Jobs: _____

_____

Why did you leave your last job? _____

_____

Special Abilities: _____

_____

## Pint-Sized Poet

Write a poem about a fly. Write a word on each blank that begins with the letter f.

There is a f _____ f _____ fly.

Who f _____ right past my finger.

I hope he doesn't linger!

**Alliteration**

## All-Around Artist

Oh the Toe-Test!

Draw a picture of a place where you would like to go if you could taste with your toes.

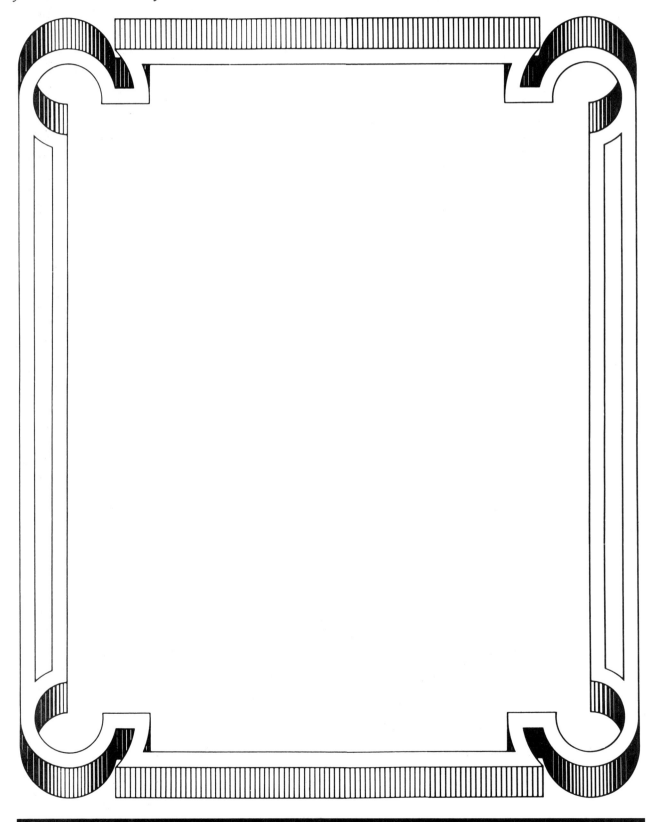

# Broccoli and Bubble Gum

## Take No Notice

If Ben has braces on his teeth
And scowls a nasty scowl,
If Joan's new glasses make her look
Exactly like an owl,
If Sammy wears a fancy tie
And red and yellow socks,
And Betsy flashes diamond rings
(Out of a cereal box),
If Bert has egg upon his chin
And down his sweater, too,
If Sal has torn her sneakers and
Her toes are poking through—
Even if Charlie comes to class
With CURLERS in his hair—
Just turn away politely.
It is VERY rude to stare.

Norah Smaridge

# Broccoli and Bubble Gum

# Writing Wizard

Take No Notice

Pretend Sammy and Betsy are talking about his fancy tie
and her diamond ring. Write what they would say to
each other on the lines inside the balloons.

# Pint-Sized Poet

Poems often have a special
rhythm or beat. Each word or
word part that is underlined
counts as one beat. Count the
beats in each line. Write the
number of beats in the box at the
end of each line.

<u>Ben</u> <u>has</u> <u>brac</u> <u>es</u> <u>on</u> <u>his</u> <u>teeth</u>

<u>And</u> <u>scowls</u> <u>a</u> <u>nas</u> <u>ty</u> <u>scowl.</u>

<u>Joan's</u> <u>new</u> <u>glass</u> <u>es</u> <u>make</u> <u>her</u> <u>look</u>

<u>Ex</u> <u>act</u> <u>ly</u> <u>like</u> <u>an</u> <u>owl.</u>

Now write your own special line
of poetry and count the beats.

_____

**Rhythm**

## All-Around Artist

Draw a picture of yourself wearing something that would make people stare at you.

Take No Notice

Name _____

# Broccoli and Bubble Gum

## Three Wishes

## I Keep Three Wishes Ready

I keep three wishes ready,
Lest I should chance to meet,
Any day a fairy
Coming down the street.

I'd hate to have to stammer,
Or have to think them out,
For it's very hard to think things up
When a fairy is about.

And I'd hate to lose my wishes,
For fairies fly away,
And perhaps I'd never have a chance
On any other day.

So I keep three wishes ready,
Lest I should chance to meet,
Any day a fairy
Coming down the street.

Annette Wynne

## Writing Wizard

Write three wishes of your own on the lines inside the balloon. Draw a picture of yourself thinking about the wishes.

## Pint-Sized Poet

Write a poem about three wishes. When you finish, you will have a poem with three stanzas.

If I found a magic lamp,

This is what I'd do:

I'd wish for _____ ,

And I'd wish for _____ .

Then I'd wish for _____

**Stanza**

For you!

## All-Around Artist

Draw a picture of something you would wish for.

Three Wishes

# Broccoli and Bubble Gum

Someone You Know?

## Is This Someone You Know?

There was a boy who skinned his knees
Jumping over his father's trees.

He took a run and he took a jump,
And down he came with a skid and a bump.

The higher the trees the higher he jumped.
And when he came down the harder he bumped.

The harder he bumped the longer the skid.
But he jumped them all. He did, he did.

And every time he skinned his knees
He jumped again—as proud as you please.

Till he tried one day to jump over the sky.
But he
        l
         a
          n
           d
            e
             d
              s
               o

*hard* it made him cry.

John Ciardi

# Writing Wizard

Someone You Know?

Imagine you are the boy in the poem. You are being interviewed for the school newspaper. Write your answers to the questions below.

Question: How old were you when you jumped over your first tree?

Answer: _____

Question: What do you like best about jumping?

Answer: _____

_____

Question: How do you jump without getting hurt?

Answer: _____

_____

# Pint-Sized Poet

Some poems have unusual shapes. Write a poem in the shape of a tree. Inside each branch, write a word that describes one of your favorite trees.

**Shape (Form)**

## All-Around Artist

Draw a picture of a special jumping suit.

Someone You Know?

# Broccoli and Bubble Gum

## Anna Elise

Anna Elise, she jumped with surprise;
The surprise was so quick, it played her a trick;
The trick was so rare, she jumped in a chair;
The chair was so frail, she jumped in a pail;
The pail was so wet, she jumped in a net;
The net was so small, she jumped on the ball;
The ball was so round, she jumped on the ground;
And ever since then, she's been turning around.

Anonymous

## Writing Wizard

Anna Elise

Pretend you are a newspaper reporter. Write a
newspaper story about Anna Elise. A newspaper story
tells *who* the story is about, *what* happened, *where* it
happened, *when* it happened, and *why*.

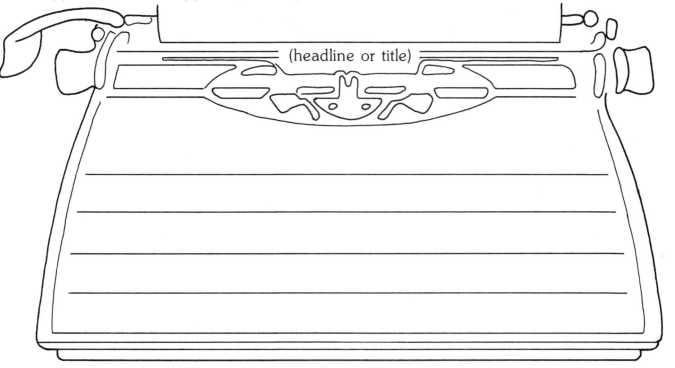

(headline or title)

## Pint-Sized Poet

Draw a line under the word that rhymes with quick.
Draw a circle around the word that rhymes with rare.
Draw a box around the word that rhymes with frail.

Anna Elise, she jumped with surprise;

The surprise was so quick, it played her a trick;

The trick was so rare, she jumped in a chair;

The chair was so frail she jumped in a pail.

**Rhyme**

## All-Around Artist

Anna Elise

Draw a picture of something that might surprise
Anna Elise.

# Broccoli and Bubble Gum

Tooth Trouble

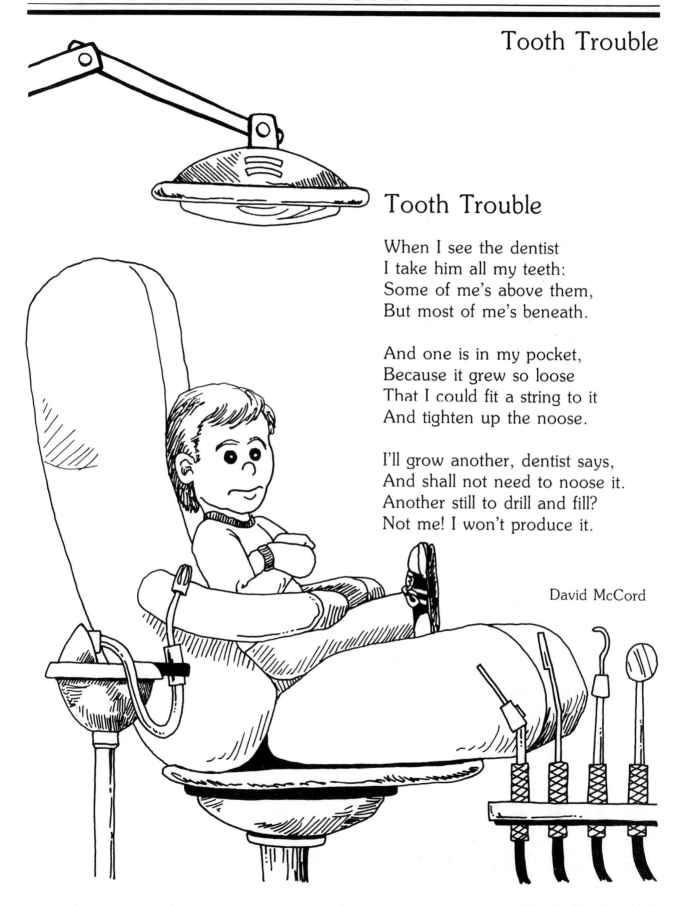

## Tooth Trouble

When I see the dentist
I take him all my teeth:
Some of me's above them,
But most of me's beneath.

And one is in my pocket,
Because it grew so loose
That I could fit a string to it
And tighten up the noose.

I'll grow another, dentist says,
And shall not need to noose it.
Another still to drill and fill?
Not me! I won't produce it.

David McCord

## Writing Wizard

Write a story about what the tooth fairy does with all the teeth that children lose.

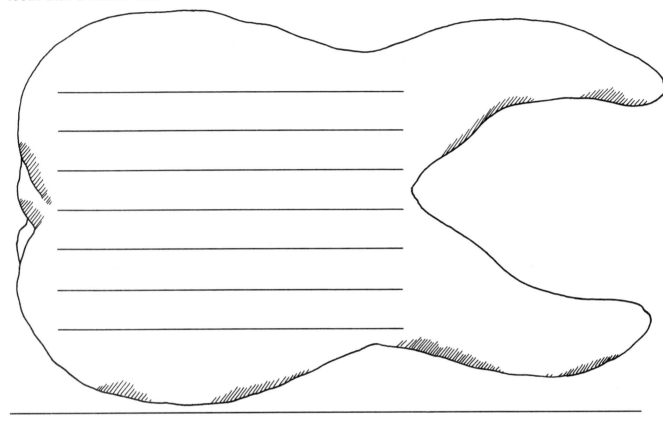

## Pint-Sized Poet

Write a poem about teeth. Write a word on each blank that begins with the letter or letters shown.

**Alliteration**

Teeth are great,

I'm sure you'll agree.

This is what

Mine do for me.

They help me:

Chew ch _____

Bite b _____

Nibble n _____

And munch m _____ .

## All-Around Artist

Draw a picture of the world's most comfortable dentist's chair.

Tooth Trouble

# Broccoli and Bubble Gum

## My Shadow

I have a little shadow that goes in and out
    with me,
And what can be the use of him is more than I
    can see.
He is very, very like me from the heels up to the
    head;
And I see him jump before me, when I jump into
    my bed.

The funniest thing about him is the way he likes
    to grow—
Not at all like proper children, which is always
    very slow;
For he sometimes shoots up taller like an India-
    rubber ball,
And he sometimes gets so little that there's none
    of him at all.

# My Shadow

He hasn't got a notion of how children ought to
    play,
And can only make a fool of me in every sort of
    way.
He stays so close beside me, he's a coward you
    can see;
I'd think shame to stick to nursie as that shadow
    sticks to me!

One morning, very early, before the sun was up,
I rose and found the shining dew on every butter-
    cup;
But my lazy little shadow, like an arrant sleepy-
    head,
Had stayed at home behind me and was fast
    asleep in bed.

Robert Louis Stevenson

## Writing Wizard

My Shadow

Pretend your shadow can take your place for just one hour. Write words of advice that you would give your shadow on the lines inside the balloon.

## Pint-Sized Poet

Write a name poem about your shadow. Write one or two words that describe your shadow on each line. Choose words that begin with the letters shown.

S _____

H _____

A _____

D _____

O _____

W _____

**Name Poem (Form)**

## All-Around Artist

Draw a picture of you and your shadow playing together.

# Broccoli and Bubble Gum

The Engine Driver

## The Engine Driver

The train goes running along the line,
Jicketty-can, jicketty-can.
I wish it were mine, I wish it were mine,
Jicketty-can, jicketty-can.
The engine driver stands in front,
He makes it run, he makes it shunt;
Out of the town,
Out of the town,
Over the hill,
Over the down,
Under the bridges,
Across the lea,
Over the ridge
And down to the sea,
With a jicketty-can, jicketty-can,
Jicketty-jicketty-jicketty-can
Jicketty-can, jicketty-can.

Clive Sansom

# Writing Wizard

Imagine you are an engine driver and you are going on vacation. Write about your vacation plans.

## The Engine Driver

Destination: _____
(Where are you going?)

Transportation: _____
(How will you get there?)

Length of stay: _____
(How long will you be there?)

Recreation: _____
(What will you do for fun?)

# Pint-Sized Poet

Write a poem about a train.

My name is _____ Train.
(name)

I race along the _____ .
(noun)

I _____ through many towns.
(action word)

My engine's painted black.

I eat a lot of coal

As I _____ with all my might.
(action word)

I like to _____ all day,
(action word)

**Personification**

And I like to _____ all night.
(action word)

## All-Around Artist

The Engine Driver

Draw a picture of a train you would like to ride in.

# Broccoli and Bubble Gum

The Sad Sliced Onion

## The Sad Sliced Onion

Once there was an onion.
The cook sliced it
And the cook began to cry
Boo! Hoo! Hoo!

The mother came to comfort the cook
And as she leaned over the sliced onion
The tears splashed from her eyes
Drip! Drip! Drip!

Then the father arrived
To comfort the mother
And he began to cry
Mrump! Mrump! Mrump!

The little boy came to comfort the father
And when he came near the onion
Tears rolled down his cheeks
Wah! Wah! Wah!

And they all cried
Boo! Hoo! Hoo!
Drip! Drip! Drip!
Mrump! Mrump!
Waaaaaaaaaaaaaah!
All over an onion.

Margaret Wise Brown

## Writing Wizard

Imagine the cook in the poem works at a famous restaurant. Pretend that you have just eaten one of his famous meals. Describe what you ate and how it tasted.

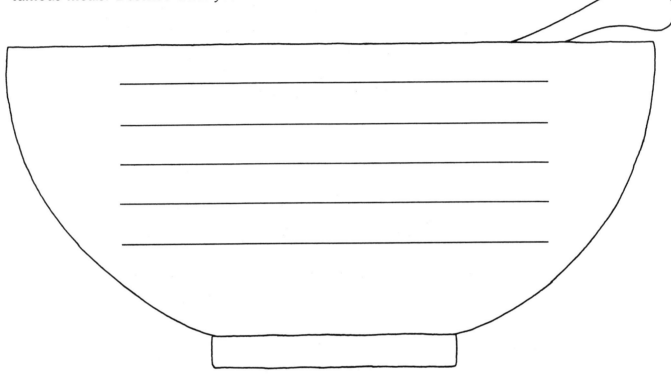

## Pint-Sized Poet

Write a poem about a silly cook. Use each of the five words listed below in your poem.

giggled          snickered
chuckled         laughed
chortled

There once was a silly cook.

She _____

and she _____

and she _____

and she _____ .

She _____ so hard

**Imagery**          that she didn't have time to cook!

## All-Around Artist

The Sad Sliced Onion

Draw a picture of everyone in the poem crying over the onion.

# ACKNOWLEDGMENTS

"Will You?" from THE BIRTHDAY COW by Eve Merriam. Copyright ©1978 by Eve Merriam. Reprinted by permission of Alfred A. Knopf, Inc.

"School, Some Suggestions" from UPSIDE DOWN AND INSIDE OUT: POEMS FOR ALL YOUR POCKETS by Bobbi Katz. Copyright ©1973 by Bobbi Katz. Reprinted with permission of the author.

"Darling Little Esmerilla" from A BAD CHILD'S BOOK OF MORAL VERSE by Charlotte Hough. Reprinted by permission of Faber and Faber Publishers.

"If You've Never" by Elsie M. Fowler. From CHILD LIFE MAGAZINE. Copyright ©1926, 1954 by Rand McNally & Company. Reprinted with permission.

Nina Payne, "Bubble Gum" from ALL THE DAY LONG. Copyright ©1973 Nina Payne. Reprinted with the permission of Atheneum Publishers, Inc.

"Jump—jump—jump" from MARIGOLD GARDEN by Kate Greenaway. Copyright ©1910. Reprinted with the permission of Viking Penguin Inc.

"When It Rains" from WINDS A'BLOWING by May Justus. Copyright ©1961 by Abingdon Press. Reprinted with permission of the author.

"Between Birthdays" from THE NEW NUTCRACKER SUITE by Ogden Nash. Copyright ©1961, 1962 by Ogden Nash. Reprinted with the permission of Little, Brown and Company.

"Sunflakes" from COUNTRY PIE by Frank Asch. Copyright ©1979 by Frank Asch. By permission of Greenwillow Books (a Division of William Morrow & Company).

"Skating" from PILLICOCK HILL by Herbert Asquith (New York: Macmillan, 1926). Reprinted with the permission of Macmillan Publishing Company.